One poem for every day
is a tall order isn't it?
What is a poem anyway?
A thought made perfect.
I am writing my life in poems.

By the same author

This Moment (2006)
Listening to Silence (2010)
All There Is (2017)

Thoughts From The Forest

Di Perry

Our Place In The Woods Publication

Thoughts from a Forest is published by

Our Place In The Woods Publications

Thoughts from a Forest

ISBN 9798499940815

In memory of my two sisters

Maddy and Eve

Di Perry was born in Yorkshire but has spent most of her life in the south of England.

She taught English as a foreign language in Italy, Greece, The Czech Republic and Moscow and has travelled extensively in South East Asia and India.

She is now retired and travels with her wife Carol in their motorhome, trying to spend the winter months in the warmer climes of Spain, Italy and Southern France. But the Spring and Summer she spends in their log cabin in her beloved forest retreat in Lincolnshire.

Contents

One poem for every day   1

December 2016   15

We planted five silver birches   17

Deep in the forest, deserted, long forgotten   19

Sweeping leaves in the forest   21

For the first time this year   22

Primroses are starting   23

The days are longer now   25

The leaves are coming out on the birches   26

I wake up at 5 am   28

Today, I walked with a friend   29

A thud on the window   30

We have a hedgehog!   31

We hear owls now the rains   32

Although it's lovely to go on different walks,   33

This plague of biblical proportions   34

There's a sadness about this time of year.   35

A deer passed through this morning   36

I am walking the long way round   37

There was a time I loved sweeping leaves.   38

A Day in the Life of   39

Walking in the lane   40

Many days I want to be alone   41

A robin is singing in the birch tree.   42

I breathe in, I breathe out, I breathe in, I breathe out.   43

A place where I am not allowed   44

In my solitude, memories come to me   45

Rain   46

How hard it is to be in the present moment.   48

The Japanese believe that negative space   49

Outside, the tree tops sway in the wind   50

Yesterday at the end of the lane   51

Leonardo da Vinci carried a notebook   52

I used to write about the past but now   53

There was a time I thought English winters were grey   54

A deer comes out of the fir trees   55

Today we walk through the snow   56

Our forest has been sold. What will it mean?   61

I walked to the little hut   62

A living tree that was leaning   63

The doors of the little hut are open   64

Today the fallen trees are being burnt   65

No deer that I can see   66

Thinking about Sartre while walking in the rain.   67

A man with two dogs   68

This seat in the forest under the oak tree   69

There is distant sound of traffic   70

The whole forest is being torn down by bulldozers   71

The wind has got up   72

Huge conifers have been thrown down   73

After bad news I walk   74

Acknowledgements   77

PART I

December 2016

We've lived in our cabin in the woods for almost a year, watching the seasons change day by day. The autumn colours are lying gold and amber on the forest floor.
The trees are majestically skeletal, stark against the wintry skies.
Birds which left us for a while in the summer for the fruits of the forest are now back from their holidays and on the feeders.
A nuthatch arrived yesterday and we have regular visits from woodpeckers, goldfinches, chaffinches, dunnocks, blue tits, great tits, coal tits and flocks of long tail tits on the fat balls which enrages the squirrels who can't get to them. So far.
Slowing down in a busy world is why we moved to the forest.
We live each day as it arrives.
We cannot change or hurry nature.

We planted five silver birches
in the boggy ground outside our cabin
C was in her element, loving it all.

Taurus. Earth.
The mud. Contact with earth.

I was not in my element.
Aquarius. Air.

I do not like the squelching.
Sinking into earth.

I changed my boots. Twice.
Turned my socks inside out.

The seams hurt my toes.
Why do socks have seams?

My grandmother knitted socks
which did not have seams.

There are so many things
I don't understand.

This morning there were robins
under the trees we planted.

Heads bobbing. Looking for worms.
I can hear them singing now.

Deep in the forest, deserted, long forgotten
a small wooden cottage next to a frozen pond
surrounded by trees, white with frost.

With a sense of wonder I stand and look,
catch a whiff of fairy tales: wolves and grandmothers,
witches and children lost in a forest.

I assume it is locked. I walk on.

Now it is spring. I walk to the little cottage
through the forest and into the clearing.
Daffodils reflect yellow in the pond

frogs have laid their eggs
trees are bright with new leaves
birds are singing and flitting through branches

I open the door. It was never locked.

Cobwebs hang like curtains from the windows
the floor is stained, strewn with newspaper
I can no longer hear birdsong

it was better from the outside,
The discovery is what gave it the magic
of a fairy tale.

Sometimes it is better not to open the door.

Sweeping leaves in the forest
swish of the broom
gently, gently,
there are primroses waiting

Sweeping leaves in the forest
I remember a temple on a hill
sounds of frogs in the night
hot smell of jungle

The enveloping dark
deep knell of an early morning bell
meditation with closed eyes
opening to red dawn

For the first time this year
I feel the sun warm on my face
The air is cool around me but the sun
Oh! the wonderful sun
is warm on my face

I can hear the chuckle of a cock pheasant
the monotony of wood pigeons
distant chugging of a tractor

There's a faint scent from
primroses at my feet
a wren is busying herself in the brambles

While the world reels
from disease and corrupt leaders
at least I have all this
and the sun warm on my face.

Primroses are starting

to cover the forest floor like yellow stars

I look into the face of one of them
for a long time

I am trying to draw it
so you can see what I see

in the humble flower
so small and delicate

I have to look intensely
Become totally involved in what is there

in order to discover lines, shapes, tones,
no erasing. The looking involves

measuring, overdrawing, changing.
At a certain moment if I'm lucky

the lines on the page will become an image
I stare at the drawing

repeatedly glance at the primrose
not at the structure now

but what is radiating from it
its energy.

I am so concentrated I can't hurry.
I take my time as though I have

all the time in the world.
I do have all the time in the world.

With this belief I continue to make
small corrections one after another

in order that the essence, the presence
of the primrose is revealed.

The days are longer now

the light evenings make me uneasy

It's not warm enough to be outside
but too light to stay indoors

There's a sense of waiting
I can't settle to anything

The leaves are coming out on the birches
trembling in a slight breeze.
The green of that first unfurling is like no other:
pale, tender, delicate. The canopy is lovely.
Like being under water.

So many cowslips growing
on banks, under trees, along the paths.
Today a new flower, a yellow pimpernel
scattered in the grass among violets
like hundreds of tiny golden stars

Every day I walk in the forest
dodging primroses, violets peeping.
Yesterday I saw a deer.
He stopped, stared, skipped on.
Around a corner, a wooden hut

next to a pond where ducks swim.
Hearing a faint cry I look up
see two buzzards swooping, curling,
floating together higher and
higher on the thermals

they seem to fly for sheer joy.
Their eyes are so sharp
they can spot a mouse from up there.
I watch them with my poor sight
until they disappear into the blue air.

I wake up at 5 am
a bird is singing outside my window

I can smell the dawn
breaking through the trees

the blind is tapping gently
on the window pane

all night while I was sleeping
life has been happening in the forest

the moon has come and gone
clouds have moved across the sky

the creatures of the night
hedgehogs, deer, owls, foxes

have been foraging for food
slugs have been eating our lettuces

now that lovely old sun has decided
to heave itself over the horizon

I will get up.

Today, I walked with a friend
to the top of the forest
and found a deer lying on the path

Her eye was bright. Her body warm.
She looked alive to me.
Better to leave her, you said gently

We walked on. But I wonder
was she alive or dead?
And if she was alive

what could we have done?
Our very presence was horrifying to her.
I like to think we did the kindest thing

to leave her to her quiet death.
But doesn't every living thing
want to know it's loved?

A thud on the window

a small bird

dead on the deck

eyes so bright

she looks alive

her body warm in my palm

so light

I feel if I squeeze

she will become dust

I bury her

in last year's leaves

under a birch tree

We have a hedgehog!

I am sitting on the garden seat
under the birch tree
watching the leaves grow dark

Behind me a rustle of leaves
and a small shape, moving steadily,
with purpose, towards me

I hold my breath as it comes close
until, rigid with delight,
 I feel its snuffling breath
on my bare foot, like a kiss.

We hear owls now the rains
have stopped at night.
How hungry they must be.

Owls cannot hunt in the rain.
Their feathers are not waterproof.
Bad design

The Little Owl with its little squeak.
The Tawny Owl with its 'terwit terwoo'.
So lonely.

They make no sound
as they swoop down on their victims.
Their flight is silent.

A hoot in the night.
Wise old owl of cartoons.
A devil of stealth.

Although it's lovely to go on different walks,

there's a lot to be said for doing the same one every day.
No walk is ever the same. Always, there's something new.
Always there's something that wasn't there yesterday.
Like tiny deer hoof prints in the mud of the outskirts of
the wood next to the plantation. I've only seen one deer
but it is exciting to know they are there in the brambles
and the undergrowth possibly watching me. It's strange
how, when once I've seen something wonderful like that, I
look for it in the same place, expecting it to be there
again. Today, violets are growing thickly amongst the
primroses. As soon as I saw one, I could see hundreds of
tiny purple faces in the grass. Everywhere is turning
green, almost by the hour.

This plague of biblical proportions

has taken us by surprise.

This has never happened in our lifetime.

We have no solution. We are stumped.

No matter which way we look

we are panicked into extreme decision.

Lock down.

Lock up.

Lock in.

We have no answers.

But still, spring arrives.

Still, birds are mating.

Still, primroses scatter the forest.

Still, bluebells lie in waiting underground.

We are of such little stuff.

A winking of an eye in the place of the universe.

I didn't know what plague was.

Now I do.

I am impressed.

I am helpless in the face of it.

Sometimes, it's better not to know something.

There's a sadness about this time of year.
The slightest breeze
brings a downpour of leaves

Suddenly
there's a chill in the air
like a warning.

A tiny wren in the brambles
the leaves scarcely trembling
as she lands on them.

I woke this morning
to a white world.
Deer footprints in the snow.

The pond by the little hut
still as glass
reflects the moon.

A deer passed through this morning

quietly under the bird feeders.

Toffee-brown, tidy. Looked back over her shoulder

at us standing inside the patio doors.

She sauntered on unafraid as though she owned the place

which I suppose she does.

A peregrine falcon visited last week

Sat for hours in the birch tree

eyeing up the birds on the seeds.

A malevolent guest. So beautiful. Bitter sweet.

I feel honoured to have him call.

But he kills the things I love.

During the night it has rained

drenching the already sodden ground.

Happy fungi grows lusciously

in clumps on the forest floor.

A summer marigold, brightly orange

glows outside my window

assuring me that even nature

sometimes gets confused.

I am walking the long way round
along the lane between the plantation
and the forest.

Squirrels are making the most
of the remaining chestnuts.
A white sun shines through the trees.

Pointing the lens I focus
and press the button
but the picture is never what I see

like the poem I feel and write
is never the real thing.

There was a time I loved sweeping leaves.
That was before my bones ached
through lifting something as light as this broom.

That was before I had to sit down every five minutes
because of my back. Now I have backache even before
I start sweeping in anticipation of aches and pains.

But sweeping leaves, I am told,
is a meditation to help me realise
the point of pointlessness.

Don't you just hate that Zen smugness
of always saying things in riddles
so even if you know you don't agree

you can't say why
because it's in the what is not being said
that the meaning lies.

A Day in the Life of .....

Today rain. Dentist. More rain.

Afternoon play. Sleep. Afternoon play.

Rain dripping from trees.

Occasional sun.

Rain dripping from trees.

Bird feeders need refilling.

Desperately trying to clear my desk.

Putting off doing the hoovering.

Tried replacing a dead light bulb.

It's stuck.

I realise I'm quite deaf in my right ear.

Old age creeps on.

Stung by a wasp yesterday.

Bastard.

Still itching today.

Bastard.

And so it goes.

Walking in the lane

sidestepping daisies, buttercups

thinking about making elderflower wine

so many elderflowers this year

and blackberry blossom

which bees love, one of which

is struggling heavy with pollen

birds are singing high in the canopy

two brown butterflies

flutter in frantic dance

everything reaching out to the sun

after days of rain

Many days I want to be alone
with just you.

Visitors are a pain in the arse
as soon as they arrive I want them to leave

but when they do leave I wish they hadn't
I panic that they may not come again.

It may happen that I will end up
with no friends at all.

A robin is singing in the birch tree.
Never mind that it's a warrior's call

daring anything to cross his space -
his whole body down to the tiny claws

clinging to the branch
is alive and throbbing with song

I breathe in, I breathe out, I breathe in, I breathe out.
Thoughts, like clouds, come and go.

Breathing in, I breathe in, breathing out, I breathe out.
Who am I?

Just another thought?

A place where I am not allowed

is always a place I want to be

the bottom of the steps
beyond the gate which says Private

What is lurking there?
It must be seen.

In my solitude, memories come to me
of a slower moving world from now.

Of waking in early morning to the song thrush
singing in the fir tree outside my bedroom window
the lawn spreading to the farm
where chickens are

Dark winters, feet cold on wood floors
silent walks to school, white breath in the air
snow ball fights
moonlight on snow

Summer sandals, white socks, brown legs,
roses in hedgerows, hair ribbons,
long days, reading days, under the chestnut tree
the green meadows of Bedfordshire lit by buttercups

The smell of smoke from bonfires in Autumn
sunsets, blackberry juice skies
darkening days, first frosts, smell of apples in the barn
salted beans in Kilner jars lining the larder shelves

All this I remember, or was it a dream I had?
Don't we all create our past the way we wish the present
to be?

Rain

It has rained for three days
by three days I mean
three days and three nights
by three days and three nights
I mean seventy two hours
maybe it will never stop
maybe it will last until the end of my life
this rain.

even the birds are fed up
and the squirrels and rabbits
the dog doesn't want to go for a walk
in this rain
this rain which has continued for three days
three days and three nights
seventy two hours

when I say rain I don't mean
that gentle drizzle that improves
the texture of your skin
I mean the rain that pounds unceasingly
on the earth, on the roof
the rain that crashes and bangs
the rain windscreen wipers

are powerless to deal with

the rain that bounces off the tarmac
the rain that batters anything
that attempts to grow
this is the kind of rain
that has rained for three days
three nights
seventy two hours.

How hard it is to be in the present moment.

Already, as I place my pen on the paper

I am in the past.

The Japanese believe that negative space
is as important as the rest of an artwork.
They have a word for it:

ma

In the silence between the notes
of a Mozart symphony
lies the mystery of music

The space between the atoms
of a thing
makes a rose, a boy, the moon

This core, this silence
is all there is
the rest is material - and immaterial

Many years ago, I went to a talk in Kathmandu given by a
Buddhist monk who spoke about the impermanence and
emptiness of all things. There is, he said, nothing that is
truly permanent and unchanging. Even the Himalayas
are moving. There is nothing that is solid matter. He took
out a box of matches and said that all that was solid in
the Himalayas would fit inside the empty box.

Outside, the tree tops sway in the wind
I can hear the wind before it arrives.
So desolate.

A sudden howling
and they start to bend and sway
Does the wind need another thing
to announce its presence?
Does it have its own sound?

When I reach the little hut
the crows are gathering -
noisily chatting about their day
orchestrating their news from the forest

A black cloud of them flies over and

suddenly

drops

into the tall trees

Hush. Silence.

Yesterday at the end of the lane

I saw a fox who saw me

He sat down and waited.
I stood still and waited.

We kind of locked together
in suspense. In anticipation.

I moved slowly toward him.
He showed no tension. No surprise.

When I got close, he looked sideways,
casually got up, turned around

and went back the way he had come.

Leonardo da Vinci carried a notebook
wherever he went.

He wrote down his impressions,
observations, inventions

But he seldom finished anything.
Did it matter?

Do I always finish everything I start?
Not always. Does it matter?

What does matter? To hear a Mozart sonata
and every note in the song of a bird

to touch my wife
and know I am loved?

Yes, that matters.

I used to write about the past but now

I write about the natural world and my relationship to it

How, what is going on inside me

affects how I see what is going on outside

Is nature beautiful only when I'm happy?

Or is it because nature is beautiful that I am happy

Does nature make me happy or am I happy first

and then see everything as beautiful

Would I have the capacity for happiness

if my world was reduced to a prison cell?

There was a time I thought English winters were grey
but today we wake to a white frosty morning

the ground a blaze of bronze leaves
each one in the morning frost has an individual life

in its white crust of rime - silver and copper.
In the evening, in the dwindling light

the trees on the plantation
are black skeletons against a red sky

A deer comes out of the fir trees
sees me and stops. Unafraid.
Delicately poised in case I
make a move towards her

she looks a long time
at me standing still
Eventually, she relaxes
her perfectly alert ears

turns her head
and dances on
stopping once in a while
to look back at me

I watch her weave
through the trees
until finally she
disappears
into
the
forest

Today we walk through the snow
around the forest. Our usual walk

The sun sparkles on white paths
and Christmas trees

Everywhere looks different.
Even as we walk it is changing

Drips from trees dimple fresh snow.
As it melts, bright grass peeps through

Deer tracks appear from the forest
then disappear back again

Yesterday I saw my first primrose
but today it is covered with snow

Two bull finches fly overhead
and settle in a tall tree

The air is crisp and clean and clear
the sky a winter blue

PART II

Our forest has been sold. What will it mean?
Things were not ideal but they were familiar.
Now changes will be made

This wild forest will be tamed, cultivated
there will be holiday makers
with children on bikes, boys with footballs

Our forest hiding places will be exposed
Maybe the little black hut will disappear
Nettles and cow parsley will give way

to manicured lawn.
There will be people on our path
around the woods. Dogs.

The small pond will be smartened up
filled with ornamental fish
There will be no wildness anywhere

I walked to the little hut
after many months away

Builders are tearing the throat
out of the forest

Trees broken.
Uprooted.

No reverence.
No apology.
No sorrow.

In Thailand, they build a small shrine
for the spirits of the land
on which they build their houses

in sorrow for the spirits
in respect for their generosity.

The spirits here must be angry.
No good will come of this.

A living tree that was leaning

has been cut down.

No trace of the branches, twigs, dead leaves.

Just a bare, slaughtered trunk.

The doors of the little hut are open
letting in the cool, clean air.
Snowdrops are growing under the trees.

I can write here. I have dreams. Visions.
 Of bringing a chair, a desk, maybe a rug
and setting up a space for myself to come every day.

I wonder who it belongs to.
It's behind a gate which says 'PRIVATE KEEP OUT' -
but there is a narrow trodden path at the side of the gate,

so it's not really private.
What does 'private' mean anyway?
It means 'It's mine - not yours.'

But as I sit here with the door open
and sweet, free air coming in -
As I sit here in this moment -

it's mine.
As I sit here within these wooden walls and breathe -
it belongs to me.

Today the fallen trees are being burnt

An enormous machine grabs the piles of branches

hauls them to the fire which stands as tall as a house

Smoke is billowing east across the golf course

there will be some disgruntled golfers choking today

No deer that I can see
in what has become my special place
No bullfinches either
although I can hear them far off in the tall trees

There is cloud, probably caused by the fire
and I think it may rain
There is no wind
The trees look bare and stark

It's difficult to imagine them green again
that inside the tiny, tight buds
there is life that in a few weeks
will burst with colour

There are snowdrops despite the carnage
but I wonder how many have been destroyed
how many small lives have been lost
for the sake of a few holiday bungalows

Thinking about Sartre while walking in the rain.

Thinking about freedom. What it is to be free.

To let go. To let go of wanting

to be free.

To be free of questions.

Let go of everything. To just be.

To understand that the only thing

is to be yourself

To follow the heart

in the face of controversy

customs, traditions, morals

This maybe is freedom.

A man with two dogs

one black, one tan

just passed me

going in the opposite direction

towards the hut

This is the first time

since I've been walking here

that I've met anyone else

This seat in the forest under the oak tree

which has become one of my shelters for writing

is here in memory of a man

who lived from 1947 to 2017

'Gone fishing' is engraved alongside his name

Who was he? What was he?

A man who fished. A man who sat beneath

this oak and dreamed

A posy of roses has been placed here.

A daughter? A lover? a son?

Someone who remembers a fisherman,

a dreamer who sat beneath this oak and dreamed.

As I do

There is distant sound of traffic

I'm trying to listen to the birds.

A little gang of long tail tits

are gathering in the oak tree

where I sit on the fisherman's seat

I can hear them munching

on whatever it is that long-tails eat

They look like fluffy pink balls

quite unafraid of me

The whole forest is being torn down by bulldozers
My green corridor is no more.

The machines ploughed into trees
pushed them down like skittles.

They have no resistance.
Their roots ripped from the earth.

Trees which breathe for us while we sleep.
Trees which give us shelter.

Trees which house animals, birds, insects.
All gone. Gone. Gone. Quite gone.

The wind has got up

since I left the cabin.

Inside the hut I can hear

the howling of the trees.

If there were no trees,

would I hear the wind?

Huge conifers have been thrown down
at the gate.
The old walk has been barred to me.
The little black hut no longer a refuge

The fisherman's seat no longer a place to sit.
To no longer watch long tails in the oak tree.
The primrose path forbidden.

This disease has created barriers
where there were none.

Where hitherto I could walk and wander,
find shelters for writing, for dreaming,
there is now fear and hostility

The little black hut is a great loss to me.
Nevertheless, I must now discover other places
in which to find the stillness I need.

It is a strange thing to come across
a barrier where none was before.
It hurts the heart, somehow

After bad news I walk
in the forest
down the new road.

Where trees have been cut down
a green corridor has appeared
into the heart of the wood

Three bullfinches, black hats,
red breasts like tiny grenadier guards
flit among the branches

Inside, two deer are standing
in a patch of sunlight
caramel coloured coats shining

I lose track of time.
They stare at me.
I stare at them.

Suddenly, one bounds away
giving a loud bark
for the smaller one to follows

I stand still, thinking about
what I have seen
when another deer, unaware

passes slowly in front of me.
There was in that moment
something marvellous

The veil between me
and the outside world
disappears. No separation.

Something that tells me
All will be well and,
all will be well.

Acknowledgements

I would like to thank the Louth Poetry and Writers'
Group for their fantastic help and encouragement in the
making of this book. In particular, Christopher
Sanderson for his endless patience and advice not only
on the contents but with my ignorance of technology and
bloody computers in general.
And of course my thanks and love to Carol for her
unfailing faith and support.

Printed in Great Britain
by Amazon